The Coming Restoration

By Kenneth E. Hagin

Chapter 1
THE NEW WAVE

Be patient therefore, brethren, unto the coming of the Lord. Behold, the husbandman waiteth for the precious fruit of the earth, and hath long patience for it, until he receive the early and latter rain.

Be ye also patient; stablish your hearts: for the coming of the Lord draweth nigh.
— James 5:7,8

James is talking here about the Second Coming. Of course, Jesus is the Husbandman. He hasn't come yet — that's quite obvious — so He's waiting for some reason or other, isn't He? What hinders Him from coming?

The Scriptures tell us why He is waiting and what He is waiting for. He's waiting for *"the precious fruit of the earth ... until he receive the early and latter rain."* ("The precious fruit of the earth" means a harvest.)

Jesus has not yet received the harvest that is to come; He has not yet received the fullness of the early and the latter rain. But I believe Jesus is coming again.

Jesus said He is coming again.

The angels said He is coming again.

The Word of God teaches He is coming again.

We have a service every Wednesday night at Rhema Bible Training Center, and every time I've been there to conduct it, I've used this Scripture from James. I couldn't get away from it. In fact, some nights as I was ready to dismiss, the Holy Spirit would say, "Well, you didn't read James 5:7 and pray, so do it." I did it. I learned a long time ago that it pays to obey God.

Many have asked, "Is there a new wave coming? Are we in that wave now? Is there more to come?" *Personally, I believe we entered into the new wave in 1982.* Certainly there's more to come.

Our text talks about "the early and latter rain." Another reference is Zechariah 10:1: *"Ask ye of the Lord rain in the time of the latter rain; so the Lord shall make bright clouds, and give them* [or send them] *showers of rain, to every one grass in the field."*

Among other things, rain typifies a refreshing or blessing. James wrote this letter to Hebrew Christians, who knew about Israel's rains. The early (or "former") rain occurred in November, after the autumn harvest, to prepare the land for future planting. The latter rain, of course, came in the spring, prior to the harvest, to mature the crop.

In times past, we've heard preaching and teaching about the darkness that will cover the earth in the last days, but I think people forget about the rest of this prophecy:

ISAIAH 60:1-3
1 Arise, shine; for thy light is come, and the glory of the Lord is risen upon thee.
2 For, behold, the darkness shall cover the earth, and gross darkness the people: but the Lord shall arise upon thee, and his GLORY shall be seen upon thee.
3 And the Gentiles shall come to thy light ...

Isaiah is really prophesying about the glorious access of the Gentiles to the Church. There's coming a manifestation of His *glory,* Isaiah says.

In Acts 2, Peter preached a sermon on

the Day of Pentecost, referring to the Lord
Jesus Christ and His resurrection. But in
Acts 3, Peter's message reached over into
the end times; it's a message that applies
to us.

In the 19th verse he said, *"Repent ye
therefore, and be converted, that your sins
may be blotted out, when THE TIMES OF
REFRESHING shall come from the
presence of the Lord."*

The American Standard Version gives
a better translation: "Repent ye therefore,
and turn again, that your sins may be blotted out, so that there may come seasons
of refreshing from the presence of the
Lord."

Let's go on reading in Acts:

ACTS 3:20,21
20 And he shall send Jesus Christ, which before was
preached unto you:
21 Whom the heaven must receive until THE TIMES
OF RESTITUTION of all things, which God hath
spoken by the mouth of all his holy prophets since
the world began.

You'll find that the Greek word translated "restitution" in verse 21 also can be translated "restoration," and it reads that way in many translations.

Notice that Peter connected times of refreshing (we often call them "revivals") *with the Second Coming of Christ. Thus, Peter taught us that times of refreshing would come from the presence of the Lord in the time of the Lord's return!*

So there are two things to notice: (1) times of refreshing, and (2) times of restoration. This passage from Acts teaches us that just before the Lord's Second Coming, we will experience both.

Some will ask what I mean by "restoration." I mean restoration of *the power of Christ,* restoration of *the authority of Christ,* and restoration of *the character of Christ.* God wants all three of these characteristics to be exhibited in the life of the Church and in the lives of individual Christians.

Christ is the Head of the Church. We are the Body. You know your head cannot exercise any authority except through your body, so Jesus is not going to personally exercise any authority on the earth except through His Church. Jesus carries out His work through the Church, but members of the Church have been so weak they haven't recognized the authority and power of the Head — the authority that belongs to them.

There are many things the Lord *wants* to do — and He's been *trying* to do — for many people, but they won't *let* Him! (I discuss this subject in detail in my book *The Believer's Authority*.)

Chapter 2
A MESSAGE TO BELIEVERS

Lately the Lord has repeatedly brought to my attention the fourth chapter of Ephesians. Paul is writing here to the Church at Ephesus — Spirit-filled believers. Notice what he said:

EPHESIANS 4:22-24
22 That ye put off concerning the former conversation [this word in Greek means "manner of life" or "conduct"] the old man, which is corrupt according to the deceitful lusts;
23 And be renewed in the spirit of your mind;
24 And that ye put on the new man, which after God is created in righteousness and true holiness.

Put on the new man!

That new man is Christ in you, the hope of glory.

That new man is the man on the inside who has become a new creature in Christ Jesus: *"Therefore if any man be in Christ, he is* [he *is,* not he's going to become] *a new creature* [or creation] . . ." (2 Cor. 5:17).

That man on the inside is a new man, created in righteousness and true holiness, as we just read in Ephesians 4:24.

Even though Paul said to "put off . . . the old man," we're still living in the flesh, and that flesh hasn't been redeemed yet. Our flesh — our body — will want to go on doing what it's always done. So how do we put on the new man, and how do we "put off" the old man? Let's read further in Ephesians 4:

EPHESIANS 4:25,26,28
25 Wherefore putting away lying, speak every man truth with his neighbour . . . [lying doesn't go with the new man]
26 Be ye angry, and sin not: let not the sun go down upon your wrath . . . [How can you be angry and sin not? By keeping your mouth shut. Anger doesn't belong to the new man; it's part of the old man.]
28 Let him that stole steal no more: but rather let him labour, working with his hands the thing which is good, that he may have to give to him that needeth.

Paul got both words in there: "labor" and "working"! He didn't say, "Let him get on welfare." You know, you could take a little side journey here and step on a few toes.

In the time of the Early Church, civil governments didn't have any welfare programs. The Church took care of its own needy, including widows and orphans. Paul, however, writing to Timothy, said that when widows had children or nephews, they should support them, not the Church. In other words, if the widows had some relatives, they should take care of them (1 Tim. 5:3-8).

We've gotten away from this; the government is doing everything; the government is almost God, you see. But Paul said the widows' relatives should take care of them. And he said believers should work with their own hands to earn their living.

We've got students who come to school

and want to sponge off the other students. They call that "living by faith." I call it "living by ignorance." They'll live with someone as long as they can.

No! The Lord told us to work. (If He told you not to work, He'll meet your needs; you won't have to be a burden to anybody.)

But we've got them every year. There are a lot of religious con people in the world. They'll con you out of everything you've got, if you'll put up with it. And some of these religious con people pick up on what they think the faith message says, but that's not what it says at all.

They want to "claim" everything you've got. One fellow tried to "claim" my red Bronco. That's coveting. If he wants a red Bronco, he can claim one, but he can't claim mine. I've still got my Bronco, and he is still walking.

A man who's living off of other people is really stealing from them. And while I'm on the subject, people who go to a church and don't put anything in — who never pay their tithes or give offerings — are stealing from the rest of the people. They want to get blessed, but they want the other fellow to pay for it.

These people need to put off the character of the thief and put on the character of Jesus. He was a *giver!*

Chapter 3
RESTORATION OF CHARACTER

Paul continued to talk about the "new man" in Ephesians 5:3: *"But fornication, and all uncleanness, or covetousness, let it not be once named among you..."* (Not only don't do it, but don't let fornication and all uncleanness even be *named* one time among you!)

By "uncleanness," Paul wasn't talking about taking a bath and using deodorant. He goes into more detail in Romans 1.

ROMANS 1:24,26-28
24 Wherefore God also gave them up to uncleanness through the lusts of their own hearts, to dishonour their own bodies between themselves [That's the uncleanness Paul's talking about.] ...
26 For this cause God gave them up unto vile affections [uncleanness]: for even their women did change the natural use into that which is against nature [It's not natural for a woman to want a woman; it's natural for a woman to want a man.]:
27 And likewise also the men, leaving the natural use

of the woman, burned in their lust one toward another;
men with men working that which is unseemly, and
receiving in themselves that recompence of their error
which was meet.
28 And even as they did not like to retain God in their
knowledge, God gave them over to a reprobate mind,
to do those things which are not convenient.

Notice that Paul uses the word
"uncleanness" in connection with lesbians
and homosexuals. He said to put away fornication, uncleanness, and covetousness —
let them not even be once named among
you.

So there must be a restoration, not only
of the power and authority of Christ, but
also of the *character* of Christ.

We need to walk in the light of the law
of love and not do things that offend other
people. Personally, I'm offended by some
of these charismatics who run around
holding a cigarette or pipe, or sipping on
cocktails.

They'll argue, "Paul said, 'Drink a little

wine for your stomach's sake.' " Well, if
you'd lived where the water was bad in
Paul's day, you might have done that, too.
But that doesn't give you an excuse to be
a winebibber today.

Even Paul said, "If eating meat that
was offered to idols is going to offend my
brother, I won't eat any meat as long as
the world stands." That's the point.

My wife and I know someone who was
an alcoholic before she was born again. She
lived a straight, strict, sanctified life for
20 years in a Full Gospel church. Then the
charismatic renewal began, and many
people from the outside, who weren't
taught to put on holiness (the character of
Christ), got into the church.

While attending a convention, this
woman went into a restaurant and saw a
charismatic minister and other Christians
drinking wine with their meal. She thought
to herself, *If they can do that, I can!* She
began drinking, and that alcoholic devil

got hold of her again. She's been an alcoholic for a good many years — bound — and can't get free.

You can say what you want to, but I wouldn't want that on my conscience when I stand before God and He says, "You caused this little one to stumble."

"But you don't understand grace," someone will argue. Yes, I understand grace. The trouble is, you don't understand the Bible.

Chapter 4
RESTORATION OF GIFTS

God's endtime plan includes a time of restoration of His *glory*, a time of restoration of His *power*, and a time of restoration of His *gifts and ministries* to the Church.

I've seen occasional manifestations of the glory of God through my years of ministry. I've frequently seen the presence of God come into the building appearing like a cloud. About four times I've seen something like waves roll in from the back of the building and hover over the people. Although it looked like waves, it was a white cloud — a manifestation of His glory.

I'm firmly convinced we're going to see more of that in these end times. We're going to move into a greater manifestation of signs and wonders than we've seen before. I believe there's going to be a revival of the supernatural.

In Ephesians 4:11, you'll find that when Christ ascended on High, He gave gifts to men: some apostles, some prophets, some evangelists, and some pastors and teachers for the perfecting — or maturing — of the Body of Christ.

Our mistake has been that we've only recognized three of these ministry gifts: the pastor, the evangelist, and the teacher. For the Church to ever be what She ought to be, and for us to have the ministry and do the work God intended, we must have the manifestation of the fivefold ministry. We must recognize the ministry gifts, honor them, and permit them to function in the way God wants them to function.

We also must recognize what we call the gifts or manifestations of the Holy Spirit: the word of wisdom, the word of knowledge, faith, gifts of healings, the working of miracles, prophecy, discerning of spirits, divers kinds of tongues, and interpretation of tongues (1 Cor. 12:8-10).

Now notice the next verse, First Corinthians 12:11, *"But all these worketh that one and the selfsame Spirit, dividing to every man severally as he will."*

Notice He is not dividing the gift; He is dividing the *manifestation* of the gift.

What we call the gifts of the Spirit belong to the Church. They have existed all the time; they have just been lying dormant. The manifestation of them is given to individual members of the Body of Christ as the Spirit wills.

We also need to understand this: Those who stand in the fivefold ministry offices are more or less equipped with some of these spiritual gifts in order to function in their offices. For instance, to stand in the office of a prophet, one must have a consistent manifestation of at least two of the revelation gifts (word of wisdom, word of knowledge, or discerning of spirits) plus prophecy.

A prophet is one who has visions and revelations; the word of knowledge operates in prophets. On the other hand, any believer may have a manifestation of the word of knowledge as the need arises.

There is going to be a renewal of the spiritual gifts. They're going to be in manifestation even more. I'm seeing it in my own ministry, and others are seeing it in theirs. (For an in-depth look at this subject, see my study guide, *The Ministry Gifts.)*

In conclusion, turn to another portion of Scripture:

LUKE 5:36-38
36 And he [Jesus] spake also a parable unto them; No man putteth a piece of a new garment upon an old; if otherwise, then both the new maketh a rent, and the piece that was taken out of the new agreeth not with the old.
37 And no man [no man!] putteth new wine into old bottles [or wineskins]; else the new wine will burst the bottles, and be spilled, and the bottles shall perish.

**38 But new wine must be put into new bottles; and
both are preserved.**

You must understand the illustration
Jesus is using. These wine "bottles" were
made of skin. Once wine was put into
them, they would swell up and change
shape. As the skin became old, it became
brittle, and if wine were put into an old
skin, it would burst.

Therefore, they would renew those old
wineskins. First, they'd soak them in
water for a long time. Second, they'd take
olive oil and rub it into the skin until it
became soft and pliable again. Then the
skins were like new again; they could put
new wine into them and they wouldn't
burst.

Jesus was saying that individuals, local
churches, or denominations often are just
like those wineskins: old, empty, dead, and
brittle.

How can we be soaked in water to be

renewed? Paul, talking about the Church, said in Ephesians 5:26, *"That he might sanctify and cleanse it with the washing of water by the word."* Washing of water by the *word!*

So there must be a fresh saturation of the Word of God. And in these latter times, God has raised up the teaching ministry for this very purpose.

Many of us, praise God, have been saturated with the Word of God. Others need to be. Unless they are, they'll never be able to hold the new wine.

We know that after they soaked skins in water, they rubbed olive oil into them until they became soft and pliable. Oil is a type of the Holy Spirit! The Psalmist said, *"...I shall be anointed with fresh oil"* (Ps. 92:10).

Fresh oil! That's what we need today: a fresh anointing of oil — the Holy Spirit — and it's coming!

A Pentecostal minister from England

visited me several years ago here in my office on the Rhema campus. He's now in his 70s. Smith Wigglesworth held a week-long meeting in his church the week before he went home to be with the Lord.

This brother told me what Wigglesworth had told them that week before his homegoing in 1947: "There is coming a move of God, but I'll not live to see it."

The English brother continued, "Wigglesworth said that the greatest move of God yet will come in the '80s." (I had always had the same conviction.) He told me that Wigglesworth said, "In our day, in this revival, we've had a move of the *gifts* of the Spirit, but very little teaching of the Word. There is coming a revival of the teaching of the *Word* of God, and after that revival comes, there will come that fresh anointing of the Spirit. And *the combination of the two revivals will bring the greatest move we've ever seen!*"

Is a new wave coming? Some people are looking for something brand new; something that has never happened before. In that sense, there's never going to be a *new* wave. God's going to do everything He's ever done before.

Go down by the ocean and watch the waves come in. You may say, "That's a new wave." Yes, it's a *different* wave from the one that came in before, but it's still the same water, even though it's higher than the first wave.

The move of God often comes in gently. But it keeps pushing in until, before you know it, it covers a whole territory.

The truth is, the new wave started in 1982. It's here now! It's gathering momentum. It's going to continue to sweep in, in even greater power — a greater move of the Spirit, power, authority, and character of God.

There's even a move of God going on in some of the Communist countries. I believe there's going to be a tidal wave of glory that's going to sweep all nations right into the kingdom in these last days!

You can receive a fresh anointing right now!

CONFESSION: Thank You, Lord, for the rain — the outpouring of the Holy Ghost — the early and the latter rain. Thank You, Lord, for the harvest — the precious fruit of the earth.

The revival is not coming. The new wave is not coming. The revival — the refreshing — is here now! And I'm in it. And I walk in it. And I'm a part of it. And I'll continue to be a part of it. And the work of God will be done.

Prophecies

Now sit idly by and recognize not the move of the Spirit. Feed not upon the Word of God. But rather walk in the flesh, fulfill the desires thereof, and you will miss entirely that which is taking place in this hour and in this day.

But respond ye unto the Word of God. Yea, soak your mind and your heart thoroughly in the Word. Let that Word not only *not* depart from thine eyes, but hide that Word in the midst of thine heart by speaking it, and practicing it, and doing it.

And then it shall be said of thee, Yea, yea, yea, yea, the Lord is my Helper and my Keeper. I walk not after man, nor after the thinking of man, nor the thoughts of man. But I walk in the light of the revelation of His holy Word. I walk in the power of His Spirit. I walk in the glory of His might. And I stand strong in Him.

And when the winds of adversity blow, as surely they will; and when the fires of persecution burn, as surely they will; and when the tongues of men shall speak against thee, as surely they will; thou shalt only smile and say, "I give an account unto the Lord. I stand before His judgment seat, and in that day I will be able to say, 'Lord, I've done my best. I've been faithful.' And He will say to me, 'Well done, thou good and faithful servant. Enter thou into the blessings of the Lord prepared for thee before the foundation of the world.' "

Yea, saith the Lord of hosts, be ye prepared. Be ye ready. Walk with Me and be sensitive unto my Spirit. Not only will thou be blessed and thy family be blessed, but thy neighbor shall be blessed, and all that thou come in contact with will be blessed; and the blessings of the Lord shall flow like a mighty river.

* * *

But many have said, "Oh, I've missed it so. I wish I could forget about the past: those mistakes, those faults, those failures, and even that terrible wrong and sin that I did."

Yea, saith the Lord of hosts, do not count as nothing my blood. Remember, my blood — precious blood, the divine blood, the blood of the Divine Son of God — was shed for the remission of sins. And, yea, the Lord has declared: I, even I, am He that blotteth out thy transgressions, and I will not remember thine iniquities.

So, do not dwell upon the past. Think no longer of that which is past. And when the enemy will bring a picture of it before your mind, just laugh and say, "Ha, ha, ha, ha, ha. That does not exist, Mr. Devil. That does not exist. Because the Father has blotted it all out, and the blood has washed it all away, and now I stand in Him!"

And the enemy may persist, but the more he persists, the more you laugh. Laugh right in his face. And he'll run away and hide, and you in the power of God, in His love and mercy, shall abide.

* * *

But some have said, "The Lord could never use me. I'm so weak and so unworthy. I've fallen so far short."

Yea, saith the Lord of hosts, do not judge yourself after the seeing of the eye of man or the judgment of the intellect of man. But rather judge yourself after the revelation of my Word. Remember that it is I, even I, who blotted out thy transgressions and refused to remember your iniquities.

That it is I, even I, who made you a new creature in Christ Jesus. For it says, "created by God in Christ Jesus" [Eph. 2:10]. And I did not make a new creature who could not stand in my presence, but would cringe from Me, run from Me, and cry out, "I'm unworthy and undone."

No, washed in the blood, cleansed by His Word, filled with His Spirit, having become His son; yea, a child of God. So come! Come boldly by the blood, even into my very Throne Room, and make your requests made known.

Realize that you belong there, and begin to be sensitive unto my Spirit that resides in your spirit, for He will guide you into all truth. He will show you things to come!

And everyone will be used of the Lord: no unused members in the Body of Christ. Everyone may not be a ministry gift *to* the Body, but everyone may function in their place. So, take your place.

"Oh," some said, "I don't know my place." Do what thy hand doth find to do. Yea, minister everywhere you go. Speak ye the Word of God, and the Word will do the work.

Yea, saith the Lord of hosts, you will not come emptyhanded; You will not be barren and fruitless; but, rather, you will come into my presence — eventually stand before my very throne — and the harvest shall be great.

And thou shalt be glad. And many,

many, many will rise up in that day and call you blessed. And a great day it shall be. Yea, saith the Lord, labor. Work while it is still day, for the night cometh when no man can work.

* * *

Think thou that thou hast seen the full manifestation of my glory? Think thou that thou hast seen the full manifestation of my Spirit? Think thou that thou hast seen the full manifestation of my gifts?

Yea, you've only seen a little: a glimpse here and a glimpse there; a little here and a little there. But thine eye shall see and thine ear shall hear the manifestation of the glory of God, the manifestation of the Spirit of God, the manifestation of the gifts of God. And thou shalt have cause for much rejoicing.

* * *

Yea, saith the Lord of hosts, do not expect the enemy to come in like a flood and overtake you; but expect the glory of God to rest upon you. Expect the Spirit of God that resides within you to function as the Holy Scriptures declare that He will function.

And He'll rise up in you and give illumination unto your mind and direction unto your spirit. For it is written, "He'll show you things to come." And you'll not ever be left in the dark, for you're not children of the darkness; you're children of the light!

And you'll walk in the light every single day. And the work of God shall be accomplished. And the glory of the Lord shall shine upon thee. And oftentimes men — that is, natural men, men in darkness — will see the glow upon thee. They'll even see the *glory* upon thee. They'll even see the *light* shining forth from thee, and come and walk with thee and be blessed forevermore.